A FAURÉ CLARINET ALBUM

arranged by Sidney Lawton

T0101048

Order No. NOV120515

NOVELLO PUBLISHING LIMITED
14–15 Berners Street, London W1T 3LJ, UK

Cover by Art & Design

No part of this publication may be copied or reproduced in any form or by any means without the prior permission of Novello & Company Limited. Permission to perform this work in public must be obtained from The Performing Right Society Limited, 29/33 Berners Street, London W1P 4AA or from the affiliated Society overseas.

© Novello & Company Limited 1980
All Rights Reserved

This copy may not be sold in France

CONTENTS

A FAURÉ CLARINET ALBUM

Arranged by
SIDNEY LAWTON

BERCEUSE

No. 1 from *Dolly Suite*, Opus 56

6

MAI

Opus 1, No. 2

rall.　　　　　　a tempo

31

36

41

46

APRÈS UN RÊVE

Opus 7

PAVANE

Opus 50

43

47

51

54

BERCEUSE
Opus 16

A FAURÉ CLARINET ALBUM

BERCEUSE

No. 1 from *Dolly Suite*, Opus 56

Arranged by
SIDNEY LAWTON

CLARINET in B♭

© Novello & Company Limited 1980

All Rights Reserved

MAI

Opus 1, No. 2

APRÈS UN RÊVE

Opus 7

CLARINET in B♭

PAVANE

Opus 50

CLARINET in B♭

BERCEUSE
Opus 16